NOAH GOES TO CAMP

"ADVENTURES IN NOAHLAND" BOOK SERIES

Written by Phyllis Leyden-Alexander ~ Illustrated By Clint Smith

Copyright © 2021 by Phyllis Leyden-Alexander

All Rights Reserved. No part of this publication may be reproduced, stored in a retrieval system or transmitted in any form by any means electronic, mechanical or photocopying, recording, or otherwise without permission in writing from the author.

Request for permission to make copies of any part of this book should be submitted via email to noahlandbooks@gmail.com.

ISBN: 979-8-9851027-2-7
Imprint: Phyllis Leyden-Alexander

Printed in the United States

To my mom, Quentine (Tina) Potter Leyden.

Until recently. I never thought much about why I've always loved to read. I now realize it's because you instilled a love for books and reading in your girls.

You read to us.
You introduced us to the Public Library as soon as we were old enough to write our own name and join.
You always had a variety of books in our home, including an old book of poetry that I consumed.

My heart is filled with gratitude.

I love you Mommy. Thank you.

The

Adventures in Noahland

Book Series

Different But The Same

Noah Goes To Camp

Noah Junior Ranger

Noah and Helen's Big Colorado Bike Ride!

Noah's Amazing White House Tour

Reviews from Ms. Marie's 3rd and 5th Graders

"It was amazing! I liked how it showed what he did and what he had to pack"
– Connor

"I thought it was cool because all the other kids at the camp also had a lot of abilities"
– Nevaeh

"It was amazing because he could do talented things that other people don't do."
– Will

"I think the story was great because even though he is different, he got to do so much along with other kids."
– Italia

"I thought it was exciting because Noah went to camp for the first time."
– Anonymous

"I really feel like it reaches out to other kids and helps me to understand what life might be like for kids like Noah"
– Carl

I think it's an overall great book with a great message and pretty good story."
– Isaac

"I liked the book because it helps people like Noah. It helps other people understand he is different, but he still has fun doing the same kind of things other kids like to do."
– Sophia

"It was a really sweet story with awesome illustrations."
– Zoey

"It made me feel grateful for the things I am able to do."
– Mia

"It makes me understand better what life might be like for Noah.
– Elijah

Visit our website, FinallyPhyllis.org, to add your child's review!

Then, out the door, down the ramp
And I'm on my way to overnight camp!

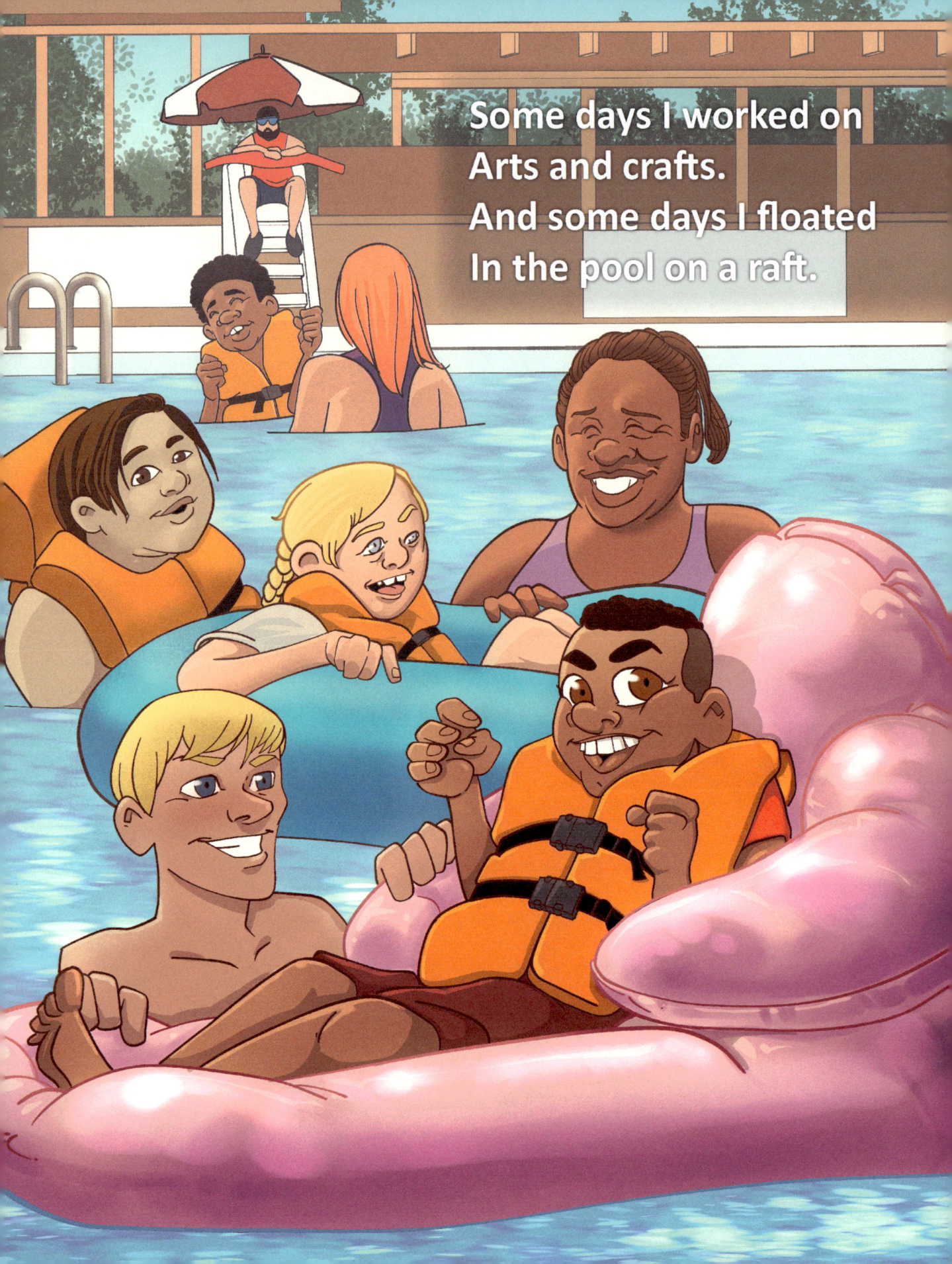

I petted animals —
A donkey, a sheep, and a goat or two.
They were all together
At the Petting Zoo.

I had two special friends,
One named Sam, one named Mike.
(Mike wore the glasses,
And Sam's hair had spikes.)

Wherever I went,
They'd also go.
On the horse, in the pool,
to the musical show.

I met lots of kids
We had so much fun.
But before long
My camp week was done.

It was time to go home,
Mom drove up in the van.
Gave me kisses and hugs,
And held tight to my hand.

Mom gathered my stuff,
Making sure all was there.
My meds, and my food,
And the clothes that I wear.

"Thank you," mom told them.
"You took care of my son.
You made sure he stayed well,
And that he had fun."

I was sorry to leave,
I wanted to stay.
But mom wanted to drive
While it was still day.

So...

To Parents, Grandparents and Guardians, from this grandmother's heart...
There's more to the story!

CAMP! Shrieked my Grandma;
No! Not overnight!
You must keep Noah near,
Not out of your sight!

What if Noah gets sick?
He will be all alone.
He should NOT go to camp.
He should stay close to home.

My mom used her calm voice,
Said, "nurses are there."
"They will keep Noah safe,
You have no need to fear."

Grandma thought for a while
About what Mom had said,
Then she gave me a hug,
And nodded her head.

See, mom's brave with the things
She allows me to do.
If I were your kid,
Would you be this brave too?

'Cause if I don't try
Then how can I know?
How great I can be
Or how far I can go.

Camp ASCCA

ASCCA stands for Alabama's Special Camp for Children and Adults. Beginning in 1976, Camp ASCCA has been a nationally recognized leader in therapeutic recreation and is known throughout the world for its superior quality services. Providing camping experiences for children and adults with disabilities, Camp ASCCA is open year-round. Within its barrier-free environment, Camp ASCCA offers 230 wooded acres on the shores of beautiful Lake Martin in Alabama.

Camp ASCCA is a special place where campers with disabilities can express their individuality and independence within a supervised setting. The activities offered at Camp ASCCA include horseback riding, swimming, canoeing, fishing, arts and crafts, accessible waterslide, zip-line, water tubing, archery and rifle range, mini-golf course, paved nature trails, splash pad and more.

The Easterseals Camp ASCCA Mission is to help eligible individuals with disabilities and/or health impairments achieve equality, dignity, and maximum independence. This is to be accomplished through a safe and quality program of camping, therapeutic recreation, and education in a year-round barrier-free environment. Visit https://campascca.org for more information.

About Noah

Noah was born 14 weeks premature. He weighed 1 lb 10 oz and was just over 12 inches long. After 22 weeks in the NICU Noah was finally strong enough to go home. I will forever remember sitting with Naomi as the Division Chief of Neonatology and several of his staff explained to us as gently as they could that Noah would be little more than a vegetable, and that we should take him home and make him as comfortable as possible. He has been diagnosed with:

- spastic quadriplegia cerebral palsy
- epilepsy – lgs
- cortical visual impairment
- bronchio dysplasis
- obstructive sleep apnea
- gerd
- osteopeneia

Fast forward, and Naomi now sums up her and Noah's life this way: "On paper Noah is a train wreck, and by medical standards he doesn't have 'quality of life'. However, Noah actually has an amazing life. It's not an easy life for either of us, yet we live out loud, are comfortable with the uncomfortable, and do everything we want and can afford. We've learned to adapt to this differently-abled ride called disability."

Today Noah is a tough, funny, mischievous 12-year-old whose mom is always introducing him to new activities and opportunities. Noah is also gaining recognition as an abstract artist, and recently held his first art exhibition at the Gertrude Herbert Institute of Art in Augusta, GA.

Noah's time in the NICU is chronicled by Naomi in her book, "And God Remembered Noah". It includes a list of resources for family and friends of those who are differently abled and is itself a great resource. You can obtain additional information on both Noah's artwork and Naomi's book at https://noahland.art.

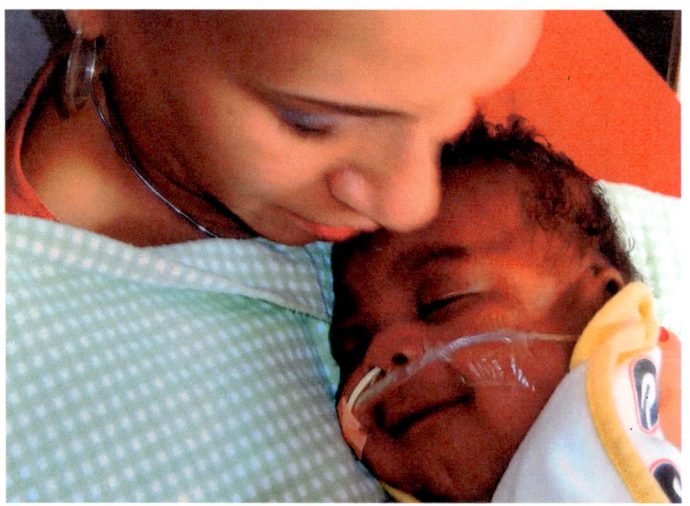

The Noahland Story

   During the summer of 2017 Noah attended an art camp with a group of typical children from several different countries. At the end of the week the kids all showed off their artwork, sharing the flags they'd made, each representing their country of origin. Upon seeing Noah's artwork Naomi said to them, "that must be Noah's flag". And one of the children piped up, "it's Noahland!"

   Noahland is actually a life full of wonder, surprises, difficulties, and achievement beyond the expectations of many. It is a glimpse into the things Noah CAN do. It is Noah being an active and visible participant in his community, living his best life, and encouraging others to do the same.

   I am continually in awe of Noah and his mom and their many adventures. It is my hope that the readers – whatever their age – will be able to come into Noah's world, get to know and enjoy him, and discover for themselves that we are more alike than they could have imagined!

About the Illustrator

Clint Smith was born and raised in Atlanta, Georgia. He grew up on a steady diet of comic books and cartoons and went to Georgia Tech where he earned a degree in Industrial Design.

He currently lives with his wife, 2 children, 3 dogs, and 1 mean cat in sunny Portland, Oregon and works as an IT Manager to pay for cat food while also freelancing in Graphic Design and Illustration.

About the Author

Phyllis Leyden-Alexander is Noah's grandmother. Born and raised in New York City, she is an entrepreneur, avid reader, and author of the first entry in the Adventures in Noahland series, "Different But The Same". Phyllis currently resides in Pittsburgh, PA with husband Louis. Their blended family consists of five adult children and six 'incredibly perfect' grandchildren, of whom Noah is the youngest.

A peek at Noah's next adventure...
Noah, Junior Ranger

Explore. Learn. Protect. The Junior Ranger pledge is recited by children around the country, each taking an oath to protect parks, continue to learn about parks, and share their own ranger story with friends and family. The Junior Ranger pledge reads: "I am proud to be a National Park Service Junior Ranger. I promise to appreciate, respect, and protect all national park areas. I also promise to continue learning about the landscape, plants, animals and history of these special places."

Come along as Noah describes what he hears, sees, learns, and enjoys during his visits to National Parks. Noah and his mom Naomi have visited over 10 parks, and with his mom's help Noah has earned a badge at each one! "This is a place where Noah can win" Naomi says, "and we can learn together".

The NPS Junior Ranger program is an activity-based program conducted in over 200 National Parks.

Made in the USA
Columbia, SC
09 February 2024

31302102R00020